POLA

by Benjamin Hulme-
Illustrated by Katie Rewse

Contents

OXFORD
UNIVERSITY PRESS

Welcome to the Poles!

Wrap up warm! We're going on a journey to the Poles.

This is the North Pole.

This is the South Pole.

The North Pole is the point that is furthest north on the Earth. The South Pole is the point that is furthest south on the Earth.

To help you understand where the Poles are, imagine you are spinning a ball on your finger. Then you put another finger on the top of the ball.

Now imagine the spinning ball is the Earth. The points where you touch the ball are the North and South Poles.

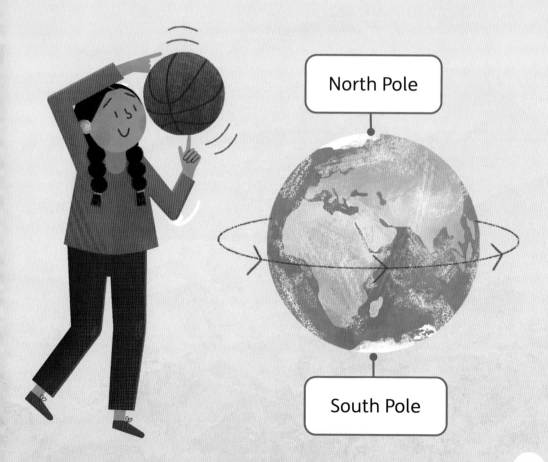

North Pole

South Pole

Cold at the Poles

The North and South Poles are very, very cold. They are covered in a thick layer of ice all year round.

It can be as cold as minus 60 degrees Celsius at the South Pole. That's over three times colder than a freezer!

Polar Wonder

These <u>natural</u> lights in the sky are called the Northern Lights or the Southern Lights. They can be seen near the North or South Poles.

The lights happen because of a special type of wind that comes from the Sun. This wind sometimes crashes into the Earth's **atmosphere**. Then it makes millions of tiny bursts of light.

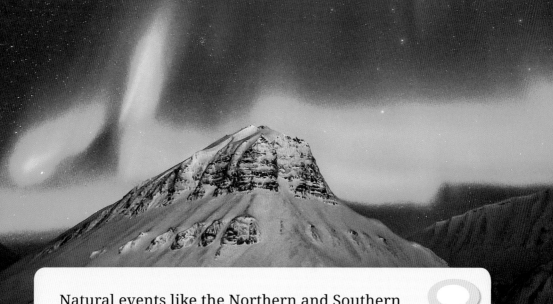

<u>Natural</u> events like the Northern and Southern Lights are caused by nature, not by people. Which of these would be a <u>natural</u> event? A thunderstorm or a firework display?

The Arctic

The **region** around the North Pole is called the Arctic.

The North Pole is not on land. It is on the ice of a frozen ocean. The frozen part gets smaller in summer when some of the ice melts. Then it gets bigger in winter when the ocean freezes again. The ice can <u>double</u> in size between summer and winter.

When the ice <u>doubles</u> in area, does it get twice as big or three times as big?

The Antarctic

The region around the South Pole is called the Antarctic.

The South Pole is on a **continent** called Antarctica. It is a rocky land with lots of ice and snow. If you went to the South Pole you would see frozen lakes and huge mountains.

Polar Explorers

It is a long way to the Poles, and it is difficult and dangerous to get there.

However, lots of explorers have wanted to travel to the Poles. They each faced a hard journey across the ice and had to deal with **extreme** weather, such as strong winds and freezing temperatures.

First to the North Pole

It is not clear who first visited the North Pole. In 1909, two American explorers both said they had got there first.

We do know that the first woman to reach the North Pole was Ann Bancroft. She was a teacher who got to the North Pole in 1986. She travelled by dog sled.

Ann Bancroft

a dog sled

First to the South Pole

In 1911, two explorers set off on different **expeditions** to reach the South Pole. Roald Amundsen was an explorer from Norway, and Robert Scott was from Britain.

It turned into a race between Amundsen and Scott.

Scott

Amundsen

Amundsen had learned a lot from the Inuit people who live in the Arctic. His team used Inuit skills to cope with the cold. His expedition went well, and he reached the South Pole first. His whole team got home safely.

Amundsen's expedition at the Pole

Scott's expedition struggled with the extreme weather. He reached the South Pole one month after Amundsen. Scott and his men did not make it home.

If someone struggles to do something, does that mean they find it easy or hard?

Ice crush

Another famous <u>figure</u> from history is Ernest Shackleton. He wanted to be the first person to cross Antarctica, travelling across the South Pole.

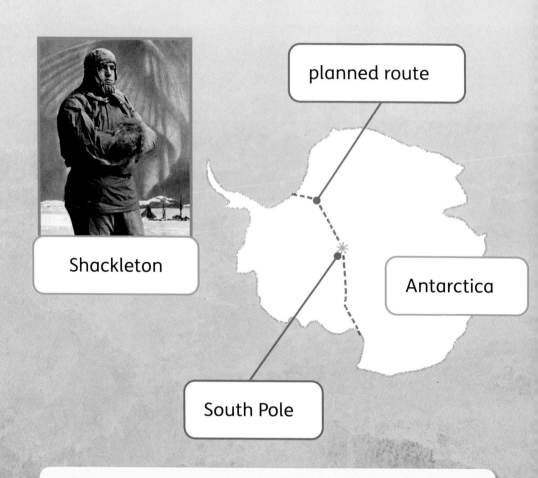

planned route

Shackleton

Antarctica

South Pole

Shackleton is a famous <u>figure</u> from polar expeditions of the past. Can you name one of the other famous <u>figures</u> mentioned in this book?

In 1914, Shackleton and his team sailed to Antarctica. Then disaster struck!

Their ship, *Endurance,* became trapped in ice and was slowly crushed. They had to camp on the ice for months before they could get home.

Endurance trapped in ice

Polar Life Today

No humans live at the North Pole itself, but lots of people live in the cold Arctic region around the North Pole. Some <u>communities</u> of people have lived there for many centuries.

A <u>community</u> is made up of the people who live in the same area. Can you think of some people who live in your <u>community</u>?

Nobody lives **permanently** at the South Pole. However, scientists often go to visit. They stay there for weeks or months at a time. They study the weather, the ice and the animals.

Scientists stay in research stations.

Arctic Hunters

Some amazing animals live in the Earth's polar regions.

Polar bears live in the Arctic. These <u>massive</u> animals hunt seals and can smell them from up to a mile away.

Something that is <u>massive</u> is very big. Can you think of any other animals that are <u>massive</u>?

Snowy fur

Polar bears and other Arctic animals have white fur to blend in with the snow and ice.

Arctic fox

Arctic hare

Arctic wolf

Antarctic Emperors

Emperor penguins live in the Antarctic. Male emperor penguins spend the whole winter out in the freezing ice and snow.

They stand in huge groups. It is coldest on the outside, so all the penguins take turns in the middle to warm up.

Emperor penguin facts

- They are around 1.2 metres tall.

- They sometimes slide along the ice on their bellies. This is called 'tobogganing'.

- They can dive down to 500 metres underwater.

- A <u>community</u> can be as large as 40 000 penguins.

- They recognize their family by their voices.

Do penguins live in big <u>communities</u> or small <u>communities</u>?

Ice Melt

Due to **pollution** in the Earth's atmosphere, the Earth is heating up. This process is called 'global warming'.

Ice in the Arctic and Antarctic is melting into the oceans. For polar animals, life is becoming more of a struggle.

If life is becoming a struggle for the polar animals, is it getting easier or harder?

Polar bears use
the floating ice
to hunt seals.

Penguins live and raise their babies on the ice.

With less ice, these animals will go hungry or
have nowhere to live.

The melting polar ice is causing big problems for people too.

To keep it frozen, we need to slow down global warming. We can all help to do this by:

- walking or cycling instead of driving

- fixing broken things instead of buying new ones

- reusing and recycling things.

The polar regions are beautiful and important.
We need to do everything we can to protect them.

Glossary

atmosphere: the air and gases around the Earth

continent: one of the Earth's seven big areas of land

expeditions: journeys to do something

extreme: very strong and not normal

permanently: forever

pollution: things that make the air or water dirty

region: area of the world

Index